Tortoise

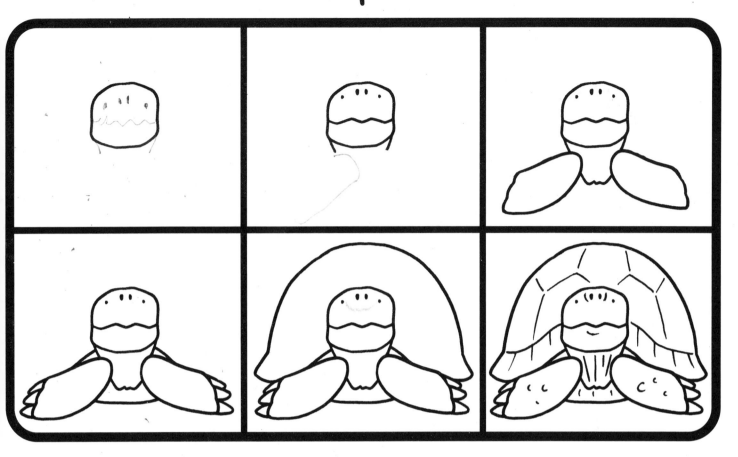

Tibetan Terrier

Peruvian Guinea Pig

Monkey

Poodle

Praying Mantis

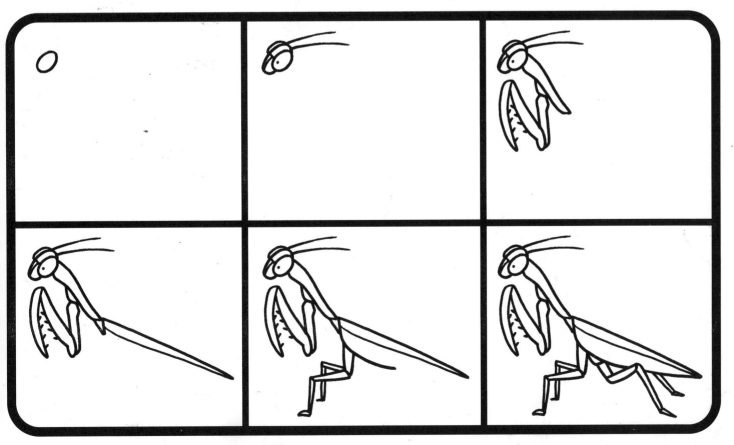

Puppy

Dachshund

Moggy

Abyssinian Guinea Pig

Rex Rabbit

Tree Frog

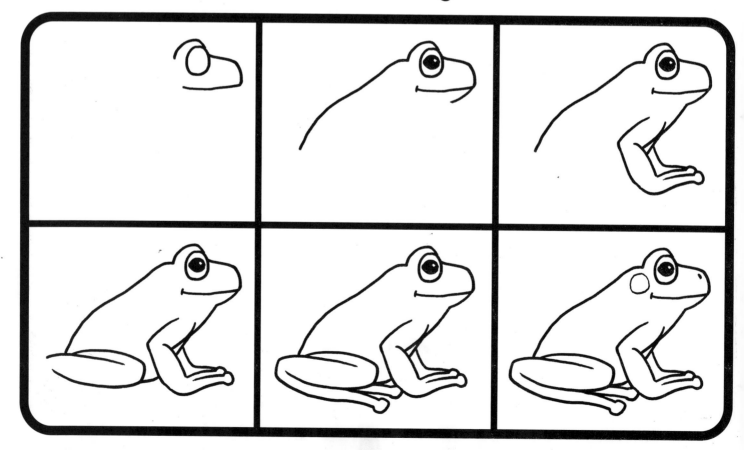

Lhasa Apso

Axolotl

White Mouse

Persian cat

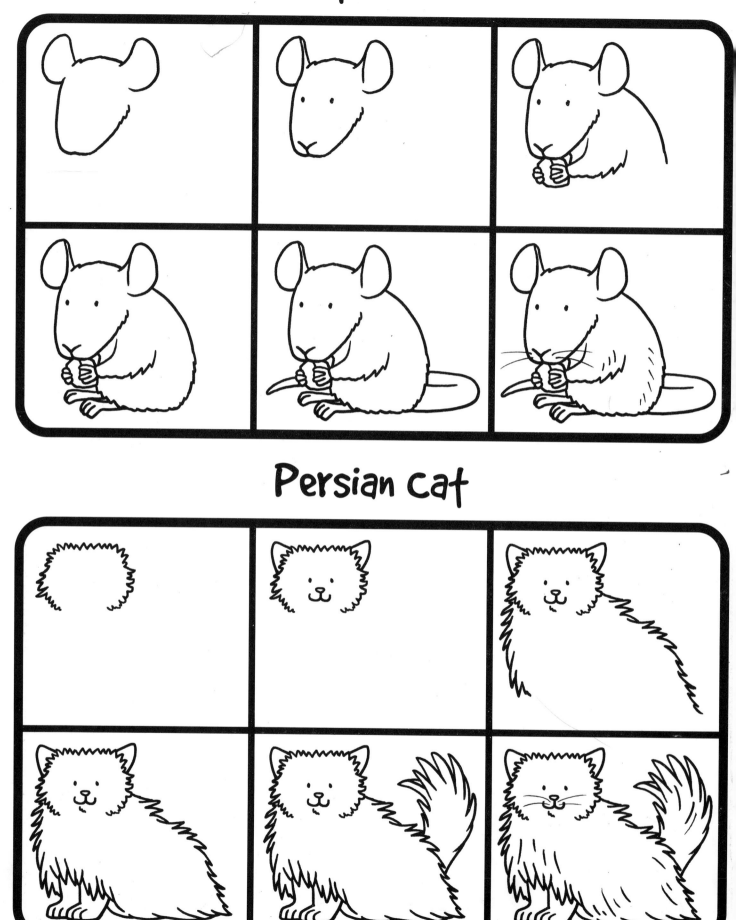

Siamese Cat

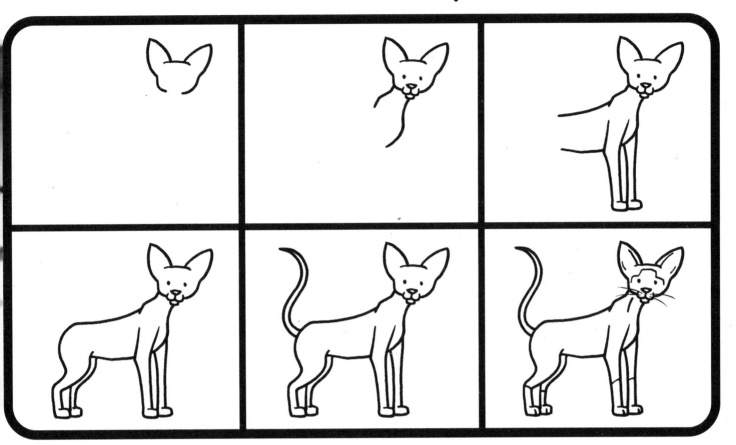

Lop Eared Rabbit

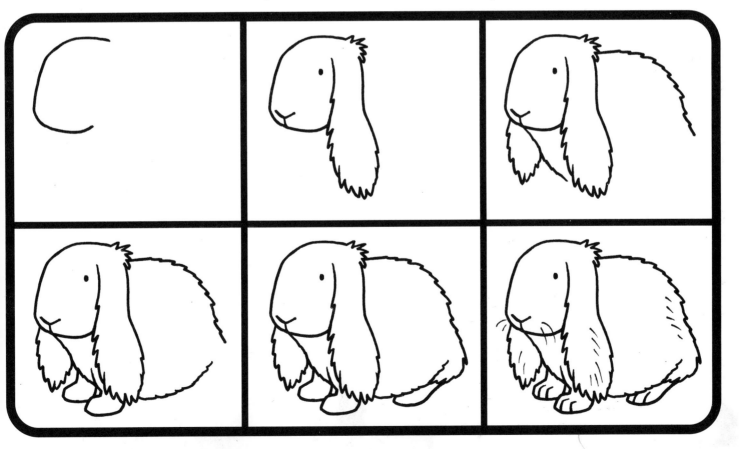

Python

Kitten

Rat

Beagle

Sea Monkey

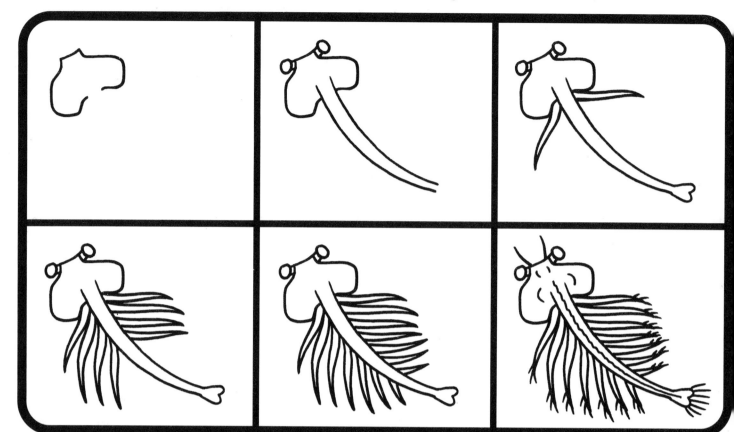

Netherland Dwarf Rabbit

Giant African Snail

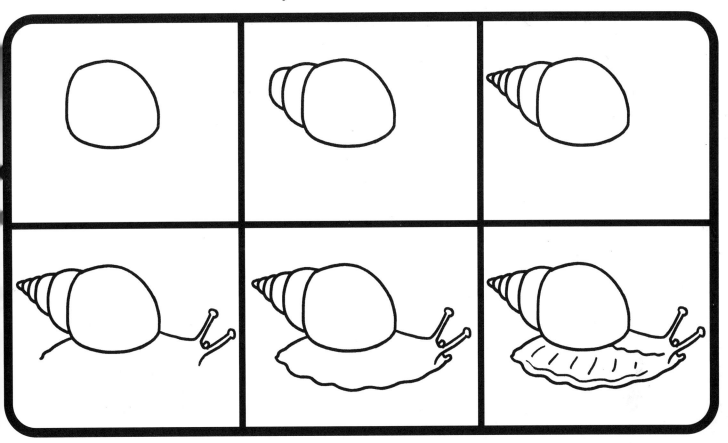

Springer Spaniel

Baby Rabbit

Angel Fish

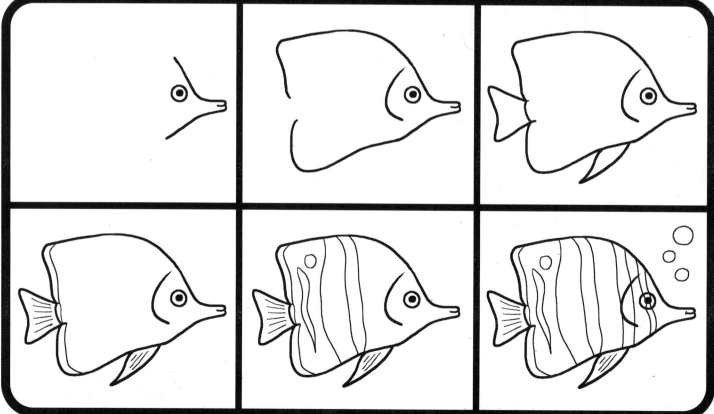

Great Dane

Manx Cat

Dwarf Lop Eared Rabbit

Bichon Frisé

Donkey

Saint Bernard

Pot-bellied Pig

Parrot

Boxer

Chameleon

Siamese fighting fish

Newt

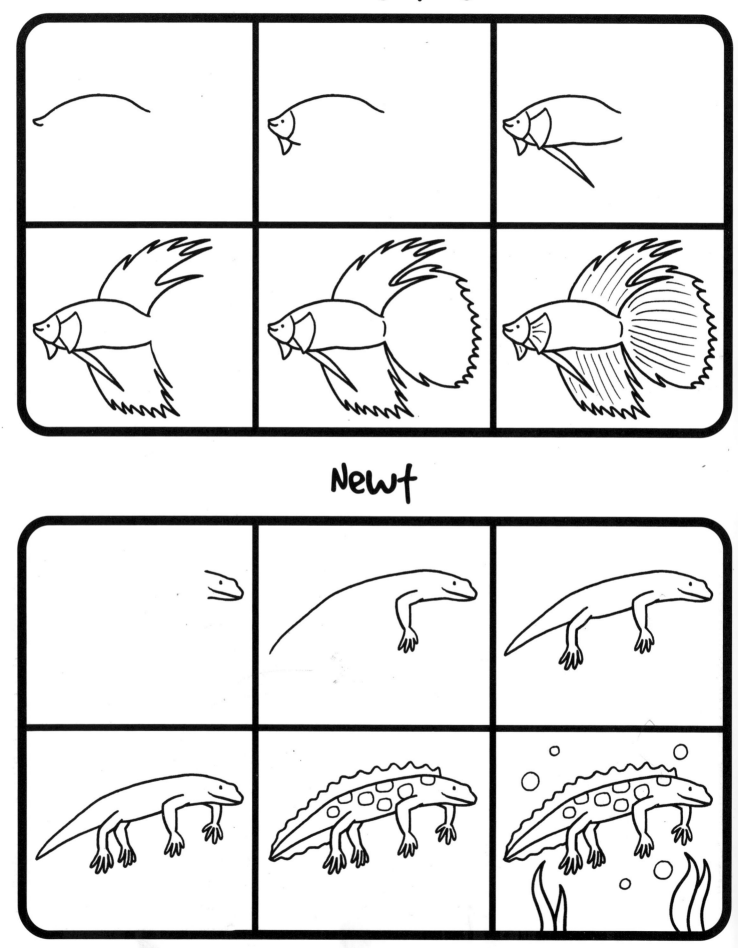

Chinchilla

Pug

Budgie

Bulldog

Milk Snake

Pigeon

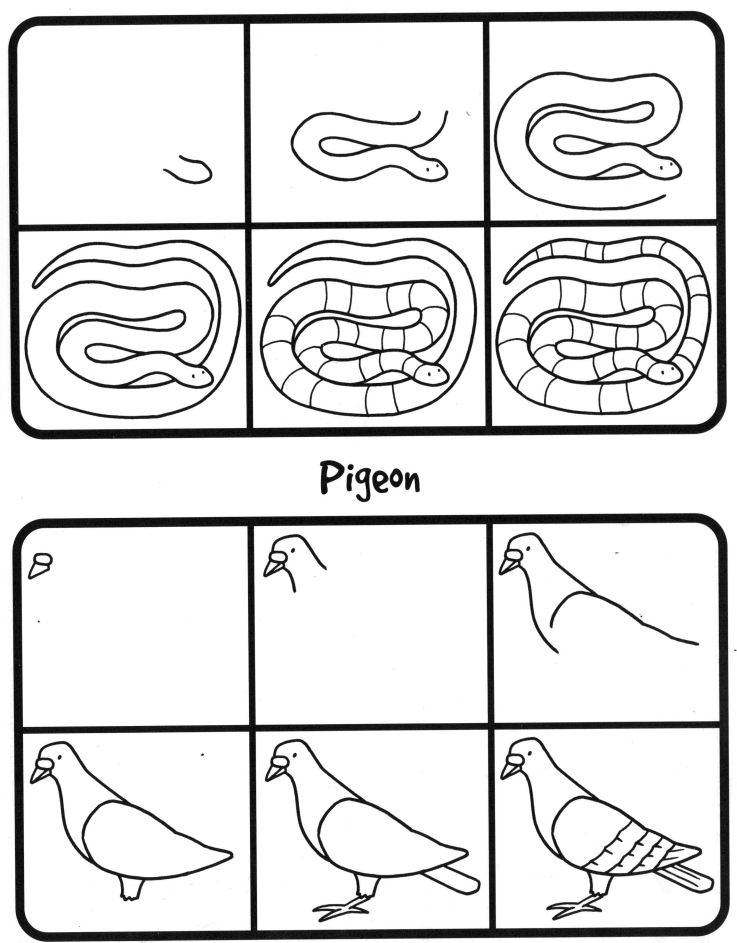

cockatoo

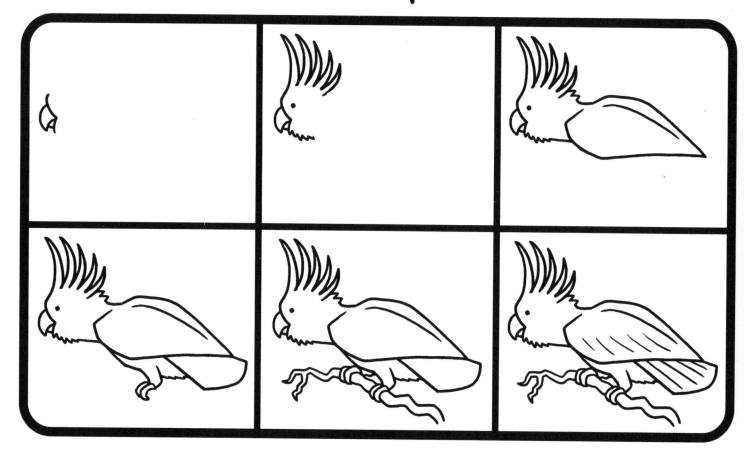

Goldfish

Long-haired Hamster

Piranha

cockatiel

Salamander

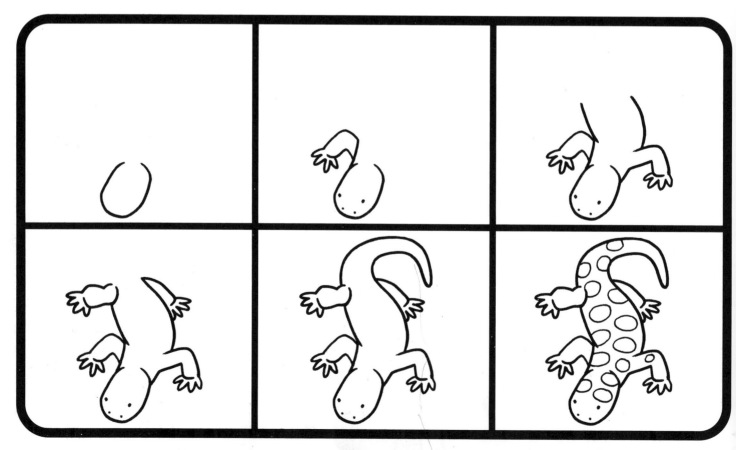

Stick Insect

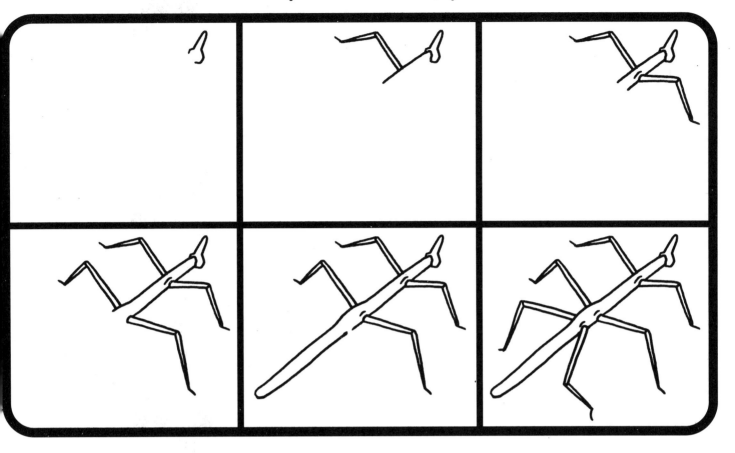

Mynah Bird

Canary

Gecko

Dalmatian

Short-haired Hamster

Catfish

Labrador

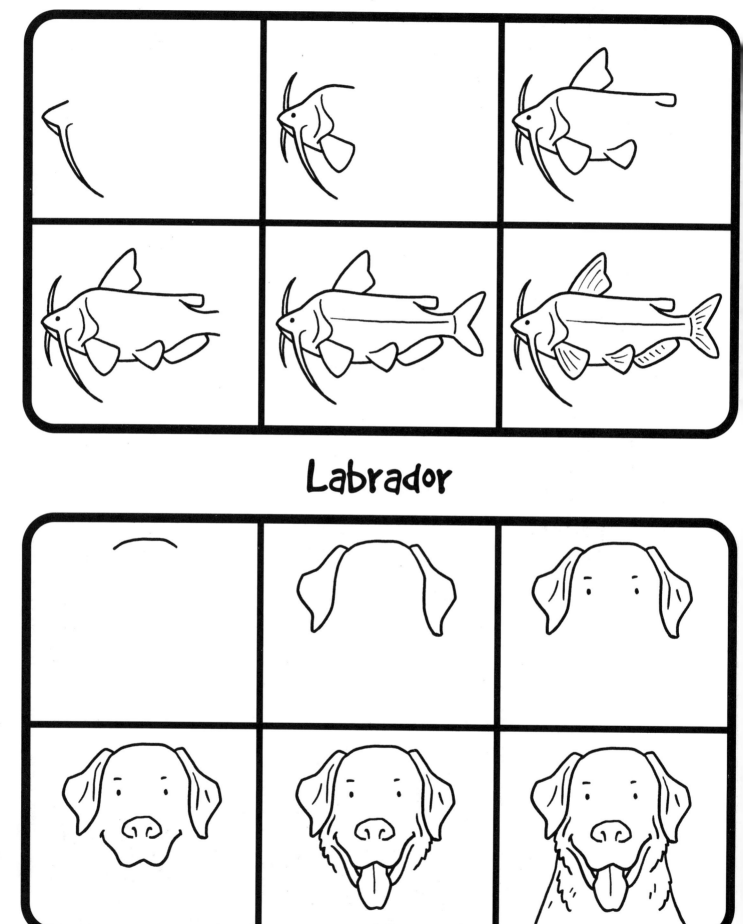

Gerbil

Hermit Crab

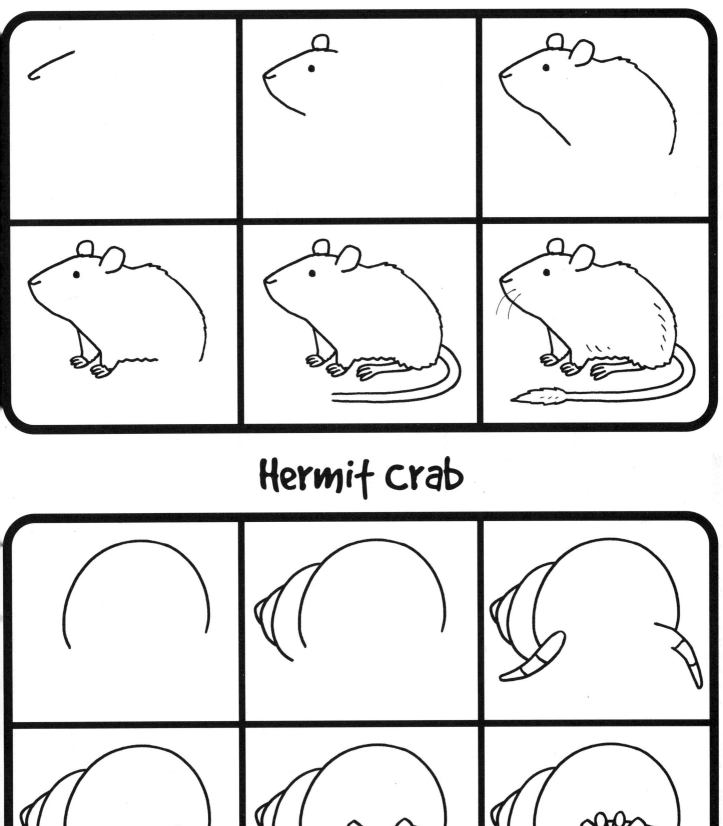

Golden Retriever

Ant

Maine Coon Cat

Russian Hamster

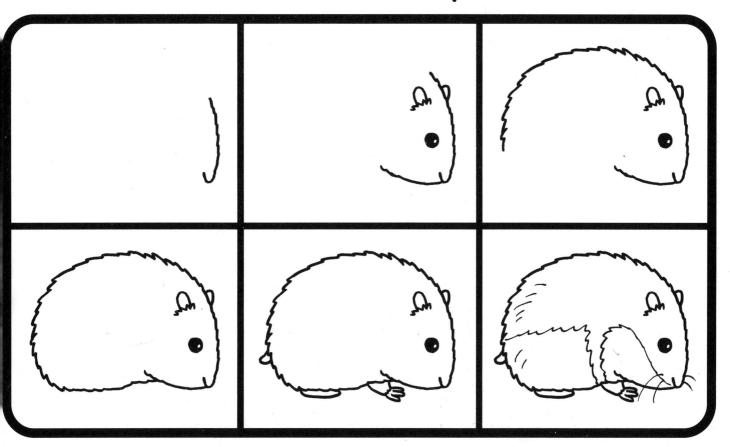

American Short Hair Cat

Bearded Dragon

Samoyed

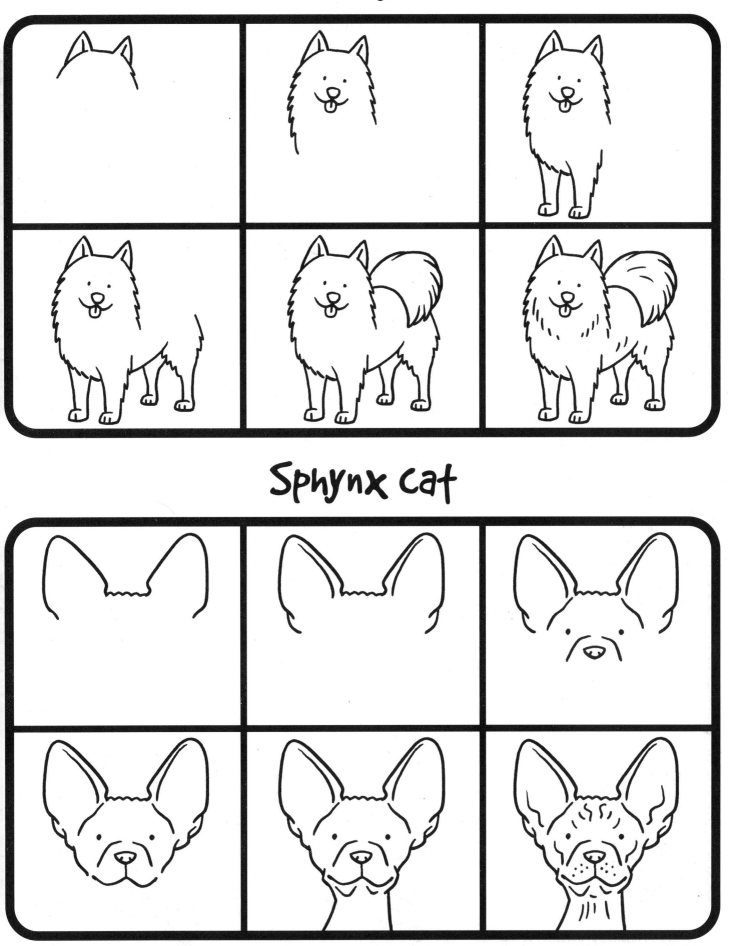

Sphynx Cat

old English Sheepdog

Tarantula

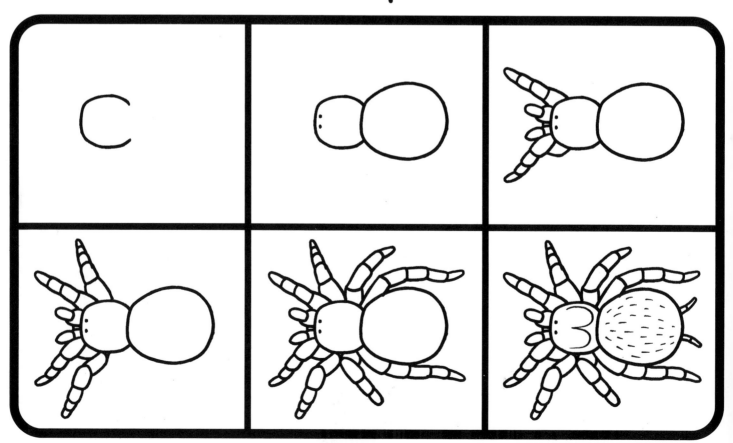

Hamster on wheel

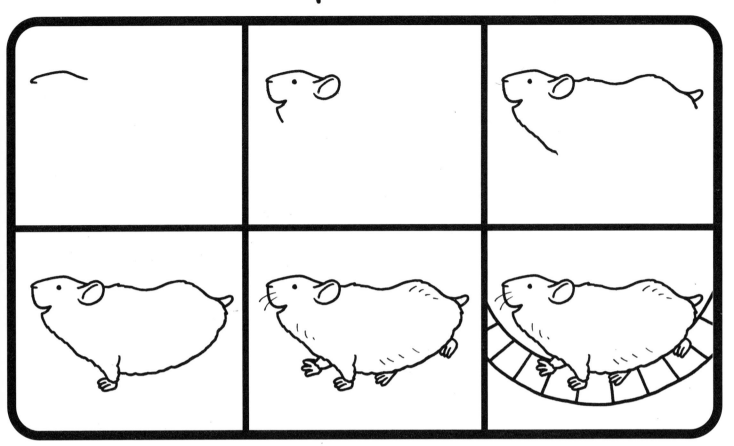

Chicken

Iguana

Frog

Egyptian Mau

Terrapin

Goat

Basset Hound

Chipmunk

Burmese Cat

Giant Millipede

Duck

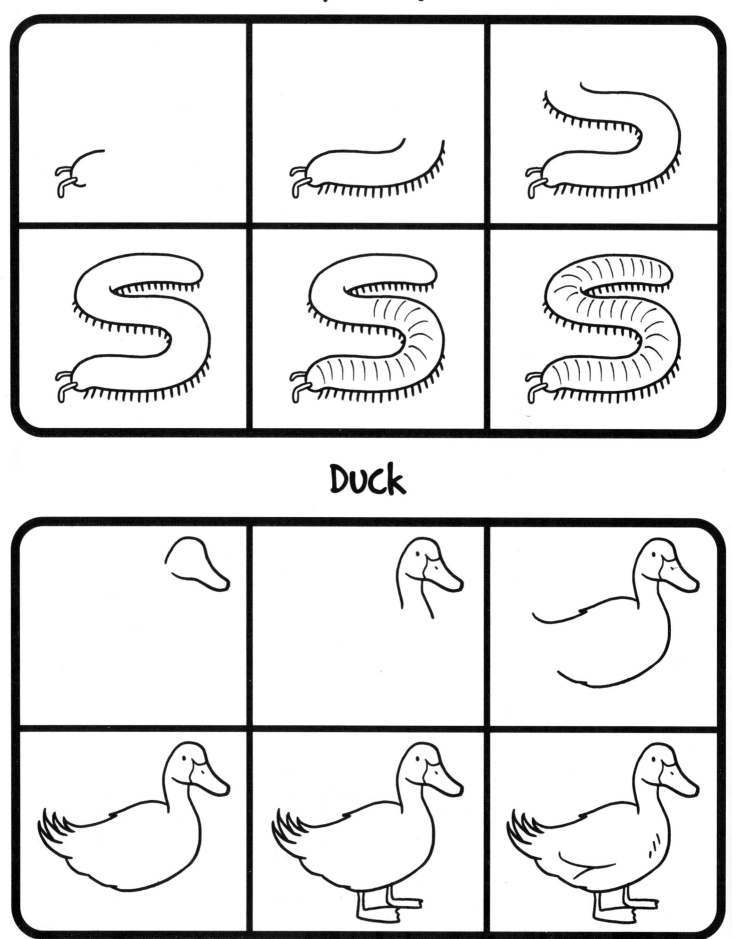

Abyssinian Cat

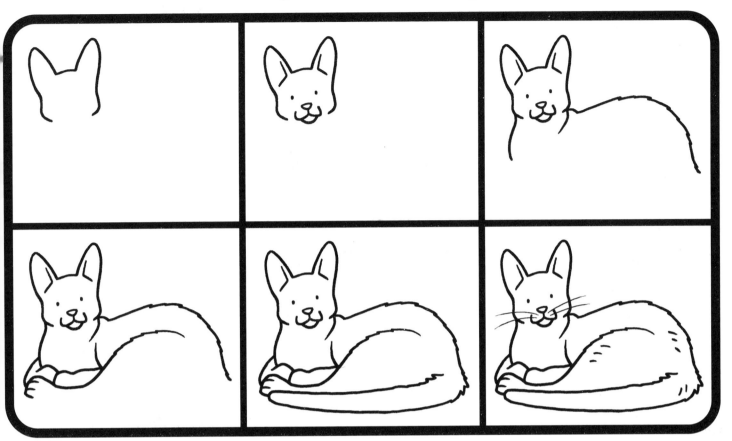

Hungarian Puli

Yorkie

Ferret

Scorpion

Alsatian

Birman cat

Shetland Pony

Clownfish

Chihuahua

Angora Rabbit

Guinea Pig

Bengal cat

Lovebirds

Ragdoll cat

Chinchilla Cat

Water Dragon

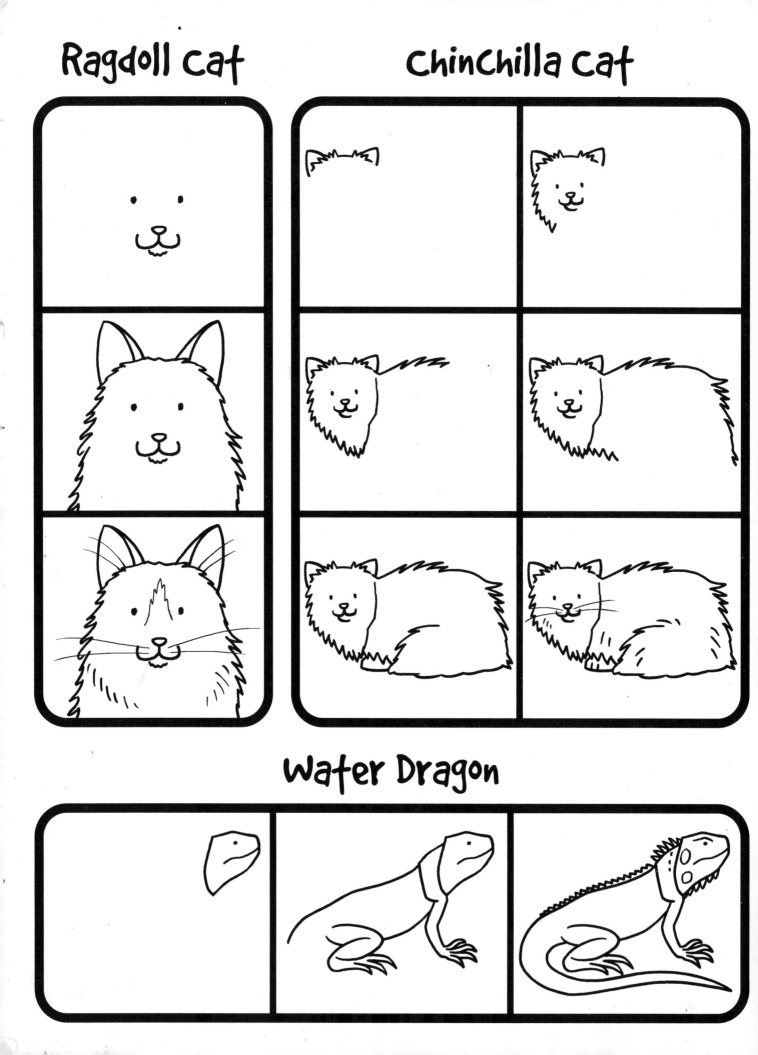